Great Britain

Cities, Sights & Other Places You Need To Visit

Copyright 2017 by Writing Souls' Travel Guides - All rights reserved.

The contents of this book may not be reproduced, duplicated or transmitted without direct permission from the author.

Table of Contents

Chapter 1 - Introduction 3
Chapter 2 - Edinburgh 9
Chapter 3 - London 15
Chapter 4 - Cardiff 22
Chapter 5 - Liverpool 27
Chapter 6 - Newcastle 32
Chapter 7 - Belfast 39
Chapter 8 - Birmingham 44
Chapter 9 - Glasgow 50
Conclusion 56

Chapter 1 - Introduction

The United Kingdom short for the UK is actually the United Kingdom of Great Britain and Northern Ireland. This is the full form of this country, which comprises of further four more countries which are:

- England
- Wales
- Scotland
- Northern Ireland

As these four countries are combined together as one under this country of the United Kingdom of Great Britain and Northern Ireland, hence the name United Kingdom is used to describe them under one heading. England is the largest of the 4 States under the government of the United Kingdom and is the meeting place of the government where the discussion of the entire country is done by the important personalities of this massive country.

About the United Kingdom and the Great Britain

Most of the people have this misconception that the United Kingdom and the Great Britain are the same and hence they are used interchangeably, by several people quite commonly. The Great Britain is actually the name given to the largest island which is located in the British Isles. This Island comprises the political identity of a total of 3 countries which are Wales, Scotland as well as England. As the Northern Ireland is not a part of the Great Britain, hence it is best for all the people to know unacknowledged the difference between the country of the United Kingdom which includes the northern Ireland and the island of the Great Britain includes the rest 3 countries but not the Northern Ireland. This is the main difference between the UK as a whole and the island of the Great Britain.

If one knows the geography well then he can segregate the confusion which lies in the fact that there are two islands which are part of the country which falls under the Great Britain, but are not physically attached to them such as the Isle of Wight which comes under England and under Scotland the Isle of Skye. The Great Britain is geographically slightly smaller than the political structure of this largest island in the British Isles. One more interesting fact about this specific topic of this place is that even though the Olympic team of the United Kingdom of The Great Britain and Northern Ireland includes the places under Northern Ireland still the team is represented by Team GB which includes all the states under the entire United Kingdom.

Ireland

Everyone has heard of the Northern Ireland, though very less people from different parts of the world actually know or has knowledge about this state. Another name of Ireland is Eire, and this entire Island stands to be the second largest of all the British Isles. The entire state is divided between the independent Republic of Ireland and northern Ireland which is affiliated under the United Kingdom.

The British Isles

A total of 6000 islands comprises of the whole of the British Isles. These 6000 Islands are situated in and around Ireland and the Great Britain. The whole area suffers from a bit of political controversy due to the fact that this does not come under any Nation as specified. Many of the people who are citizen of these islands never introduce themselves as British citizens due to decibel political controversies offering between the Great Britain with the Ireland.

England

England is the largest country under the countries which comprises of the Great Britain. This country spreads far and wide and takes almost two third of the entire area. England is surrounded by water bodies all around it. The Atlantic Ocean on one side of the silence and the North Sea and the Irish Sea on the other two sides, the nearest land is the mainland of Europe. The main town and cities of England is comprised of much smaller area compared to the rest of the island which is covered with rivers hills mountains and lakes. Such scenic beauty makes this island look like a paradise.

England has approximately 51 million citizens living in the country. Most of the population of this country resides in London, which is the capital of England. Divided into 9 regions England is one of the most beautiful countries in the world.

Wales

Wales is one of the countries which comes under The Great Britain as well as the United Kingdom. It is located on the west side of the country of England and this approximately of the size of Massachusetts, which is in the United States of America. The capital of this country is Cardiff and the whole country's population is approximately 3 million. The whole of Wales is divided into 5 parts which are Northwest, North East, Mid Wales, South East and South West. It is quite well known among the tourists for its jagged coastal regions and beautiful mountain clad national parks. Wales is one of the most modern coastal cities of the world with an extraordinary night life scenario combined with the Celtic culture and medieval castles.

Scotland

Scotland is situated in one of the most beautiful landscaped areas in Europe. This is not only creative and innovative in its own way, but the people here are also immensely kind hearted and welcoming in nature. The population of Scotland is 5 million estimated and the capital city is Edinburg. The largest city of this country is Glasgow. This country is a perfect combination of diversity in culture along with a vast source of natural resources and exhilarating landscape.

Being one of the most vital parts of the United Kingdom it captures almost the entire one third of the northern region of the Great Britain. It comprises of 800 small size Islands which also includes the famous Northern Isles of Orkney, Shetland, Arran, Hebrides along with Skye.

Chapter 2 - Edinburgh

About the city

Edinburgh is not only the capital city of Scotland, but also is a notable city that leads the globe in terms of the unique summer festivals like the Edinburgh International Festival and the Fringe, which are held here. It is a World Heritage site as acclaimed by UNESCO and a melange of both history and the contemporary. Lying in the Lothian regions of Scotland or the Scottish lowlands, close to the estuarine region called the Firth of Forth; the city offers exquisite tourist attractions. From historical heritage sites like the Royal Mile, the Palace of Holyrood House in the Old Town of the city to enthralling nightlife, appetizing food offered by a few Michelin star restaurants, along with a quaint extinct and a prehistoric volcano called the Arthur's Seat; Edinburgh presents unparalleled places to visit for certain.

Besides, Edinburgh is also the seat of the Scottish Parliament as well as the Scottish monarchy. It is the second largest financial centre in the UK and has been and inspiring centre for the cultivation of education, ranging from diverse fields like sciences, medicine, literature, the Scottish system of Law as well as engineering. It is the home to several significant buildings and institutions like the General Assembly of the Church of Scotland, the National Museum of Scotland, the Scottish National Gallery, and the University of Edinburgh and so on.

Travelling facilities to and from the Edinburgh Airport

Through the Edinburgh Airport, the entire nation of Scotland meets with the remaining world. It is the busiest airport in the city of Edinburgh and is located in the area of Ingliston. There is a wide variety of transport options from the airport to the heart of the city.

- **By taxi**

One can avail from two sorts of taxi facilities from the airport. Firstly, one can pre-book the official and the private taxi facilities by contacting with the official department of Edinburgh Airport. Secondly, one can also hire a regular black cab from the multi-storey car parking area.

- **By bus**

The Airlink Bus Service is easily available to any tourist from the airport which hops both at Murrayfield Stadium along with the Edinburgh Zoo. The buses ply 24 hours a day and all the seven days a week. It takes about half an hour to reach the city centre by bus from the airport. They run at a frequency of 10 minutes.

- ***By tram***

Travelling by tram also takes about half an hour like the bus services. They are available between 06:18 hours and 22:48 hoursand are available every 7 minutes from the airport. Alongside the city of Edinburgh the tram service offers halts at several places like St. Andrew Square, Edinburgh Park, Edinburgh Gateway and the like.

- ***By car***

A number of companies operate and offer hiring options from the airport to the centre of the city. The private car hiring saves about 5 minutes of time than the bus and tram services respectively. The cars opt for the A8 Glasgow Road and travel about 12 kms from the airport to the city centre reaching one within half an hour.

- ***By train***

The Scottish train service connects the entire nation along with the U.K. brilliantly and thus opting for a rail ride from the airport is not only very convenient but also is a fantastic way to brood over the exuberance of the city. Since there are two railway stations, Waverley and Haymarket, located conveniently at the heart of the city, one may avail their destination by rail as per one's itinerary.

Significant places to visit in Edinburgh

Edinburgh is a captivating tourist place appealing to a variety of tastes of a variety of tourists owing to its diverse range of places of utmost significance. Covering an area of about 264 square kilometres, Edinburgh, with its charismatic aura proves worthy enough to be considered as one of the finest and choicest cities of Europe. Some of the very popular tourist sites in the city are:

Edinburgh Castle

The Edinburgh Castle is a must visit for tourist and is unsurprisingly the most visited tourist spot of all in the city. The castle is atop an extinct volcanic plug, Castle Rock and on the Royal Mile and offers a panoramic view of Edinburgh. One may notice several other tourist attractions inside this castle, such as St. Margaret's Chapel, The National War Memorial and so on.

Edinburgh Zoo

The city zoological park, popularly known as the Edinburgh Zoo, is not only a perfect place for children's visit but an intriguing one for adults as well. This zoo is the abode of more than a thousand species of creatures like koalas, pandas, flamingos, chimpanzee, penguins, etc. Several eminent zoologists deliver interesting and inspiring speeches in here for the awareness of the general mass about the wild life.

The National Museum of Scotland

This place beholds the showcase of a wide range of arts and artefacts representing diverse cultures around the world along with intriguing exhibits of the natural world.

The Scotch Whisky Tasting Experience:

Whisky enthusiasts, especially ones who have a knack for relishing Scotch whisky must plan for being a part of the whisky making procedure in the city by enrolling their names with The Scotch Whisky Experience.

Camera Obscura

Among the most popular places to visit in the city, one must not forget to visit the famous Camera Obscura. It is a marvelous creation of 1853 offering tourists the engaging and fun of optical illusion. Camera Obscura is located on the Royal Mile.

Calton Hill

Similar to the Acropolis of the Athenian origin, the Calton Hill is located at the city centre appearing to pierce through the Scottish sky imparting wonder in the minds of the tourists.

Arthur's Seat

The Arthur's Seat is a snow capped summit of an extinct volcano belonging to the prehistoric era and is a popular leisure hiking destination among tourists as it takes only 45 minutes to cover starting from Holyrood.

The Royal Botanic Garden

The Royal Botanic Garden of Edinburgh is a sprawling landscape of about 72 acres and offers Victorian glasshouses and beautiful canopies of delicate floral trees like azalea and rhododendron.

Chapter 3 - London

About the capital city of England

London has a verity range of cultures and people, and more than 300 languages are spoken in this place. London is one of the leading city in the world from every place like education, arts, commerce, fashion, health care research, etc. It is counted as the world's largest financial centre. London is the first city to host modern summer Olympic games in 2012 three times. London contains four beautiful heritage the Tower of London, Kew garden, Westminster Abbey and St Margaret's. London underground is the oldest underground railway connection network in the world. London is the capital of England, which is most populated and United Kingdom. London has the fifth or sixth largest GDP in the world. London was one of the most populated city from around 1831 to 1925. As measured by the International arrived it was one of the most visited city.

Transport facilities from airport to city

Five major airports are there present in London, which has several flights from all corners of the world flying to and from this city. There are many options for airport transfers in London which you can avail.

- ***Opting for Train***

Train is available at frequent intervals from the airport to central London. Heathrow Express runs within every 15 minutes between London Paddington station to all five Heathrow terminals. Heathrow connect service runs from London Paddington to Heathrow central, terminals 1,2and 3. 25 minutes is the journey time. Stansted express takes approx 47 minutes to go between London airport to London Liverpool Street in the heart of the city. 36 minutes to Tottenham Hale. Gatwick express runs between London Victoria and to South terminal station every 15 minutes.

- ***Look for Private Cars and Cab services***

You can easily book a private airport transfer through Golden tours for up to eight passengers. The taxi or car driver will pick you up from any London airport. There are several car services ready to avail from budget vehicles to luxury ones which is easily available from and to every London airport.

- **Selecting the Famous Tube Service**

If people want to travel to or from Heathrow or London City Airport you can also use your Oyster card and take the tube. The Tube facility will guarantee you fast travelling at an affordable cost.

- **Hire a Car**

If you want to drive the car by your own in the central London, you can easily book a car at airport. You can also find out information on where to park your car and information about parking in London.

Tourist attractions place which you cannot miss in London

If you visit London then you must visit the mentioned places given below so that you can feel the rich culture of this city to the fullest extent. London has a long list of tourists spots which makes the people visiting this city mesmerized and take their breath away.

Westminster Abbey, London

It is located near the house of Parliament, is more a historical site than a religious site. The Abbey serves as the burial ground for many sovereigns, artists and politicians. Many of the coffins even stand straight due to lack of space. In this place approximately 3300 people are buried in the church. There is a grave of an unknown warrior of World War l when worries died on the battlefield in France and was buried in France soil. From 1066 every royal anointing, special cases of Edward v and Edward VIII has taken place in the church.

Warner Bros. Studio Tour

Different types of sets, costumes, props from the film Harry Potter series, is situated at the back of the screen walking features. It is located at the studio where it was filmed. It helped the film to explore the magic in the studio. It also opens the hidden secrets, which also includes the facts about the special effects and animatronics which made the film hugely popular in the world.

Hop on hop off bus tour

Bus covers 4 different routes with more than 50 stops, which gives you the opportunity to see London's most famous places. You can easily hop on and off this bus gives you the opportunity to explore the areas in details. An audio or live tour guide is present in the bus who guides you. WiFi is also available on this bus.

Great Britain

The Coca-Cola, London Eye

It is located in the heart of the London, it is rotated over the Thames river opposite the House of Parliament and big Ben. It is one of the world tallest cantilevered observation wheel with 135 meters. It is one of the Morden symbols representing capital and global icon. It will lift you high enough to see up to 40 kilometres on a clear day.

The view from the Shard

It is designed by Master Architect Renzo piano, it has become the London's iconic symbol of the London. Height of 800feets, it allows the visitors to see as far as 40 miles. Double as high as any other vantage point in the city, it the one of the best place were visitors can see the entire city at once.

Kensington Palace

It is influenced by generations of royal women, a place of secret stories and public lives. It has a remarkable painting from the Royal collection. It helps you to experience the life of the 18th century royal place by making your place through the magnificent Kings and Queens state. Fashion rules, styles this exhibition was influenced on three royal women the Queen, the princess Margaret and Diana. This collection includes the dress worm by all three women.

The Tower of London

You will discover the history of royal place despite this place is known as a place of torture and death. An armory and powerful fortress. Learn about the wild and wonderful animals that have inhabited the and the royal beasts, it makes the first London zoo.

The Buckingham Palace

These attractive rooms are decorated and designed with some of the old treasure from the royal collection, which also includes the painting of Reubens and Canalettos. In the summer you can visit 19 iconic state rooms. They host a special exhibition in the summer each year.

Madame Tussauds London

It has elegant and incredible history with more than 300 attractive and outstanding wax model. You can enjoy the walk on the red carpet with Benedict Cumberbatch and Johnny deep, before traveling through the sports zone includes Usain Bolt and David Beckham, you can enjoy an audience with the Queen and will and Kate, before going on the stage and enjoy the music with Miley Cyrus. This place will also relive the rich history of London.

Great Britain

The London Dungeon

These places are uniquely thrilling attraction that will take back to the pasts more horrified bits. London darkest stories come to life before your eyes you can see, hear, feel and smell the situation. You will understand and will go face to face with frighteningly funny characters, from tortures and judges to local legends. As you will hear the Story you will feel yourself in different worlds, where the line of reality and the past blur.

Chapter 4 - Cardiff

About the city

The city of Cardiff is a wonderful discovery for tourists for its sparking and gallant bay amidst the city of Wales. Popularly known as the "Capital City of Wales", Cardiff is the eleventh largest city in the United Kingdom, the largest city of Wales and has been ranked sixth by the National Geographic Channel as an alternative tourist destination. Metropolitan in nature, the city offers a maritime climate to visitors owing to its convenient location in the northern temperate zone. Be it the 'Capital City of Wales' or the 'Castle Capital of Wales' or even the 'Sports Centre of Wales', no epithet completely defines the glorious Cardiff which outshines several globally popular cities with its vibrant dynamism in spite of being just a country town.

Wanderlust tourists would find a diverse array of places to visit here; from the colossal Cardiff Castle to the globally famous Principality Stadium along with tempting offerings of independent cafes and shopping arcades of Victorian panache and of course, the romantically relaxing waterfront, this Welsh city is a lucrative package for wayfarers from around the world.

Transportation facilities to and from the Cardiff Airport

Cardiff Airport is seated in the Vale if Glamorgan in the Rhoose area. It is the only international airport in Wales, which is at a distance of about 19kms from the city centre and it takes about half an hour at most to cover the distance by car. The T9 bus shuttle is the most opted for transportation medium for its convenience and availability, however, other options are also plentiful.

- **Travelling by train**

The nearest railway station from the Cardiff Station is the Rhoose Railway Station, which can be reached via 905 shuttle bus service within a span of about 10 minutes. Trains ply at an interval of an hour between Monday and Saturday, however, on Sundays, they run at an interval of 2 hours.

- **Travelling by bus**

The most convenient of all is the T9 bus service maintained by the official department of the airport itself plying to the city centre starting from 05:00 hours every early morning. The tickets need not be bought beforehand and are meant to be purchased on the bus itself while being assured to be reached within 30 minutes.

- ***Travelling by car***

Using the postcode CF62 3BD, one may follow the navigation by satellites and opt for the junction numbered 33 on the M4 for getting access to the main domain of the airport.

- ***Travelling by taxi or being dropped off by visitors***

Opting for a private drop off may cost a slightly steep fare of about 30 Pounds by taxi and again, one is given a span of 10 minutes for being dropped off by visitors. Exceeding 10 minutes in case of such a drop off by visitors is charged at a rate of 5 Pounds per 10 minutes.

Must visit places in Cardiff

The Welsh capital is the Garden of Aden for sightseers centering the 11th century Cardiff Castle, which imparts a majestic vibe to the city life. Besides, the city lures wayfarers on budget to roam about the city uninhibitedly on foot to explore from the wide range of cafes, pubs, shopping plaza, historical buildings, spas, boutiques and so on.

Great Britain

Cardiff Castle

The Cardiff Castle is a Victorian splendour and a historical romantic fantasy and is prominently located in the heart of the Welsh capital. Having been a witness for about 2000 years, the castle stands with pride for sheltering not only the genteel Bute family but also noble and heroic knights. Architecture William Burges, known as for his eccentric genius, created an opulently lavish poetry with the construction of his marvelous monument. At present, the castle has opened its gates to visitors to relish the secret passageways and tunnels that once served as a confidant to World War II survivors.

National Museum Cardiff

The National Museum Cardiff opens at 12:30 hours and has at least a single thing to offer two different kinds of visitors; from housing paintings and sculptures that are about 500 years old to the largest living leatherback turtle and mammoth size skeletal remains of a humpback whale, along with showcases of natural and national history, the museum is a priceless gem in the crown of the city.

Principality Stadium

Owned and maintained by the Welsh Rugby Union, the Millennium Stadium, currently known as the Principality Stadium hosts several nail biting sports events and is a must visit for all; This arena has been Speedway Grand Prix of Great Britain and several rugby and football matches along with significant musical concerts.

The Norwegian Church

The Norwegian Church is a quaint little church close to the Cardiff Bay and invites visitors to relax on the patio of the amiable café that the restored church has set up. This church had witnessed the regular visit from the eminent literary personality, Roald Dahl during his childhood.

The Doctor Who Experience

The Doctor Who experience is a very popularly craved visiting spot among young adults and olds owing to the sets of the series that was shot here. Visitors get to enjoy nerve wrenching action videos, costumes and artifacts and the undeniable presence of a TARDIS.

Wales Millennium Centre

The Wales Millennium Centre is a true representative of the culturally rich Welsh city. It stages performing arts like modern dance, opera, circus, ballet, musicals, and so on. The authority, of late, allows visitors to relish tours to the back stage to enjoy behind- the -screen fun.

Mermaid Quay

The Mermaid Quay is an exotic waterfront cherished by both locals and visitors as it is a perfect venue to get refuelled after a hectic day of monotonous daily life or rigorous sight-seeing respectively. The place is not only a paradise for shopaholics but also a gift for foodies. From traditional Welsh cakes and ice creams to exotic Turkish meze or even the cheesiest Italian style stone pizza, the Mermaid Quay, almost at a stone's throw from the city centre, is a wonderland for all ages.

Chapter 5 - Liverpool

City of Liverpool

Liverpool may be termed as the fifth largest metropolitan area situated in the United Kingdom. It is a city located in the North West London. It is situated on the eastern side of the famous Mersey Estuary. In the year of 1880 it became a city and followed by the year 1889 it was county borough which was independent of Lancashire. The merchants of the city were engaged in the Atlantic slave trade along with handling general cargo, raw materials like the coal and cotton, freight, etc. This port became the major port of departure for the English and Irish emigrants in the 19th century. The two famous football club teams Liverpool and Everton is situated in Liverpool, if there is a match between these two teams then it is termed as the Merseyside derby. The namesake club of the city is the sole British club to win five European Cups.

Transport facilities for to and fro from the city
- **About the Liverpool Airport**

The direct air connection across Europe and United Kingdom is done by the Liverpool John Lennon Airport which is situated in the south of the city. On the present day the airport services to 68 destinations, where Berlin, Barcelona, Paris, Zurich and Milan are also included. This airport is generally served by the low cost airlines, but still charter services are provided during the time of summer.

- ***A Port facility for you to travel***

The Britain's one of the largest port is the port of the Liverpool, which provides ferry to the passenger from the Irish sea to Belfast. A cruise terminal made its appearance in 2007. Later on Liverpool2 was opened, which is an extension to the port and it allows Post-Panamax vessel to dock at Liverpool.

- ***Rail links to travel faster***

Liverpool has two railway networks, one is run by the Merseyside and the other is managed by Network Rail. Network Rail connects Liverpool with other major towns and cities of England. The primary mainline station of the city is Lime Street station acting as a terminus for many lines into the city. This station provides a link with London, Preston, Manchester, Nottingham, Norwich, Birmingham. On the Southern part of the city, a connection is provided to the airport by the Liverpool South Parkway.

Places of attraction which you cannot miss

Hearing the name of Liverpool the first two things that come to mind are The Beatles and the Liverpool football club with their famous Anfield Stadium. There are also other things to explore in Liverpool they are the Albert Dock, Merseyside Maritime museum, Pier Head, St George's Hall, Walker Art Gallery, Liverpool Cathedral, Birkenhead Park, Museum of Liverpool etc.

The Beatles

Liverpool is the birthplace of The Beatles. There are many tours which offer fans to follow the footsteps of The Beatles. They visit The Beatle shop and also a Mc Cartney's home where The Beatles use to write and rehearse.

Anfield stadium

The Anfield Stadium, where the Liverpool players, practice is also one of the places of attraction where many tourists who are football lovers finds interesting. The tourist finds attraction in seeing the ground, the tunnel from where the player come out and also the dressing room of the Liverpool players.

Albert Dock

This was the first facility built in Great Britain, it is made up of bricks and iron and is a five storied building. It is surrounded by harbor basin where previously cotton, sugar and tobacco was unloaded. Albert Dock also contains The Beatles Story Museum, where photographs and films of the Fab Four are present. It also has the Border Force National Museum which describes the story of smuggling during 1700s to the present day.

Merseyside Maritime Museum

It is a fascinating exhibition which describes how thousands of emigrants left for North America from Britain via Mersey between the time of 1830 to 1930. The artifacts of the seafaring in Liverpool are also present in the museum. It also illustrates history with the help of workshops, model ships and historic vessels. It also has the U-boat-Story that describes the life, spending in a submarine during the wartime.

Pier Head

Three Graces are the traditional trio of the harbor building which contains The Cunard Building, The Royal Liver Building and the Port of Liverpool Building. It's a great place to roam and hang around. Many people often found in taking photos.

St George's Hall

It is a great hall consisting a large organs which are used for concert purpose. The prominent Liverpudlians statues are present on the rear side of the building.

Walker Art Gallery

It is an art gallery consisting of the masterpieces done by Rubens, Rembrandt and Rodin. Outside London the English paintings and statues of 18th to 20th century is unrivaled.

Great Britain

Liverpool Cathedral

This Liverpool Metropolitan Cathedral says about the Irish origin living of the Liverpudlians in the city. The Irish emigration took place in the 19th and 20th century, where many immigrants settled in this city. Construction of the building started in the year 1928 and the whole work was finished in the year of 1967. There is a huge tent of 200 feet diameter, which surrounds the cylindrical tower which rises, ending up in a funnel shaped drum.

Birkenhead Park

On the Western side of the Mersey lies the Birkenhead which is connected to Liverpool by means of tunnels and the Mersey Ferry service. Birkenhead Park may be regarded as the first park which was funded publicly which was opened in the year 1847. It basically has three entries, namely Gothic, Norman and Italianate architecture and also composed of an ornate bridge and two lakes. People also find this place more interesting because of the Williamson Art Gallery which consist the first-rate collection of pictures and porcelain.

Museum of Liverpool

The Museum of Liverpool was opened in the year 2011 and it describes the unique geography, culture and history of the city. There are many archaeological remains, photos, decorative art and objects which represents the social ad urban history of the city. The Lion Steam Engine which was built in the year 1838 is also presented in the museum.

Chapter 6 - Newcastle

Newcastle is a city of North East England, in Tyne and Wear which is situated on the north bank of Tyne River, 446 km north of London and 166 km south of Edinburgh. It is the capital of northeast of England in both cultural and economic sense. Forming the core of Tyneside conurbation, it is one of the most populated cities in the North East and also stands in the eighth position as most densely inhabited city area in the United Kingdom. It was a part of Northumberland till 1400 and retained itself as a country till 1974 then it became a part of Tyne and Wear is a currently also a member English Core Cities Group. Geordie is the dialect and regional nickname for people from the Newcastle area, it is also home to Newcastle University.

Transportation System from this city

Newcastle has the largest transportation system in Tyne and Wear which consists of bus network, metro system and an international airport, the commuter transport executives who is accountable for transport in Tyne and Wear are called Nexus. The metro connects Sunderland to Newcastle and also other boroughs as it is one among the total of two cities in the United Kingdom to have an urban metro system outside London. The metro has two lines, Green Line connects South Hylton to Newcastle Airport via Sunderland, Gateshead and Tyne city centre. The yellow line connects South Shields to St James via Jarrow, Gateshead, Whitley Bay, Tynemouth and North Shields. The Newcastle railway station is an eminent stop on the East Coast Line and is operated by different companies. In the United Kingdom the tenth busiest airport is the Newcastle Airport.

Top Sightseeing Spots In NewCastle
The Tyne Bridge

The Tyne Bridge is one of the seven bridges crossing the Tyne River and is the most iconic and renowned which links Newcastle to Gateshead and Tyne. It was designed by an engineering firm named Mott, hay and Anderson and was later constructed by Dorman Long and Co. It was the longest single span bridge in the world when it was being built. It started in 1925 and was inaugurated by King George V in 1928. In the month of September as a part of the Heritage Open Days, the tower of the Bridge is opened for public. The Great North Run is conducted on the Bridge annually, which makes it more recognized as escorted by a display from the Red Arrows around 52,000 runners pass the Tyne Bridge.

Historic Quayside

Currently, most of the old house working as shops, restaurants and hotels, the Quayside district situated around Tyne and High level bridges has been redeveloped. The Merchants' Court and Guildhall along with many other historic buildings can be spotted on Sandhill. With a refurbished Jacobean front, Bessie Surtees House has two merchant's houses for 16th and 17th centuries. Victoria Tunnel is a 2.5 mile long captivating underground visitor attraction which is below the city from the Tyne to the Town Moor. As a wagon way to export coal from the colliery to the riverside jetties, the Victoria Tunnel was opened in 1842 and a bigger section can be explored by a guided tour. Seven Stories and Life Science Centre are nearby attractions for kids.

Newcastle Castle

New Castle's construction begun in 1080 and finished by 1172, and is situated on the St. Nicholas Street in the north of Newcastle's High Level Bridge. The King's Chamber and the late Norman Chapel can easily be visited to discover the castle's many medieval chambers and old passages. Many captivating archaeological artifacts can be spotted along the way, it also offers an excellent view of the city. The gate house which is also known as the Black Gate is also worth exploring which was constructed in 1247. During themed seasonal events, guided tours are also available to visit both the structures.

St. Nicholas Cathedral

With having a remarkable feature of lantern tower St. Nicholas Cathedral stands 197 feet tall with a top of the beautifully crenellated Scottish Crown. It was constructed in 1435 and has been given a promoted status to cathedral from a parish church in 1882. It stands at the Mosley Street. During the night time the top is floodlit with mesmerizing effects. Numerous excellent statues dating 15th to 20th century, the organ dating 1676, lectern and canopied front from 1500 are the highlights which are included in it. A very good café is also present there to refresh your mood. The work of Sir Alfred Gilbert from 1900 was the statue of Queen Victoria is also present outside in the St. Nicholas Square.

The Old City Chares

The Chares, one of the oldest regions of Newcastle are on the east side of the Tyne Bridge. It is a series of well preserved narrow lanes and medieval streets with stepped lanes there is a lot of fun to discover, it includes Long Stairs, Castle Stairs and Breakneck Stairs. The Castle Stairs lead to the Black Gate and Castle Keep. The Trinity House built in the year 1721 and the Custom House built in 1766 can also be spotted along the way. Built in the Neoclassical style, All Saints Church can also be explored which was constructed in the 18th century by David Stephenson above the tombs of Roger Thronton and his wife. Standing on the Akenside Hill, the Catholic Church has mahogany woodwork along with the biggest brass in England.

Grey's Monument and Grainger Town

The 135 feet tall Grey's Monument stands at the northern end of the Grey Street, which is a favorite meeting place in the centre of the city. It was built in the year 1835 to commemorate second Earl Grey, who was the architect of the 1832 Reform Bill and the Prime Minister. Seldom open to the public, the viewing platform of the column is a 164 step climb which offers the best views of the city. Grainger Street ends at Grey's Monument, which is also most crowded shopping street of Newcastle. Named after the architect Richard Grainger, Grainger Town is named after the architect who rebuilt the city centre from 1824 to 1841.

Laing Art Gallery

Constructed in 1901, the Laing Art Gallery contains wide collection of sculptures and paintings including paintings by artists like Stanley Spencer a British from the 20th Century, landscapes by John Martin and Gaugin. It also proudly holds sculptures made by Henry Moore and arts like ceramics, glassware and silver from 16th to 18th centuries. The gallery is also home to educational activities and temporary exhibitions. Hatton Gallery at Newcastle University holds works from the 14th to 18th century with artwork made by European painters as well as English artists.

Jesmond Dene

Jesmond Dene is undoubtedly among the most beautiful parks in England, which is linked to Armstrong Park and is situated in the northeast of Newcastle. Millfield House near the entrance of the park is the place which offers different activities and information. A nature trail laid out in mid 1700s takes tourists past the Old Mill. Gibside, a forest garden in Burnopfield is also worth discovering as it is known as the North's best landscapes. Gibside also features numerous walking pathways, Column of the Liberty and a Palladian chapel. A totally working steel making furnace from the 18th century, Derwentcote Steel Furnace is also nearby to explore.

Chapter 7 - Belfast

About the city

Belfast, the capital city of Northern Ireland, as described by the native language, means the ' river mouth of the sand banks' and is a budding cosmopolitan city. It is the largest city in the Northern Ireland and the second largest one in the entire island of Ireland covering a sprawling area of about 115 square kilometres and is one of the busiest industrial cities in the world owing to its considerable participation in the realm of global trade and commerce. Situated on the banks of River Lagan, Belfast is governed by the local council, Belfast City Council and is noted for its remarkable quality and production of characteristic Irish tobacco, Irish linen, ropes and ship building. Home to two airports, George Best Belfast City Airport and Belfast International Airport, the city can be toured conveniently, not only from different zones of Ireland but also from different parts of the globe. Belfast has become a significant location for shooting the famous fantasy political dramatic series, Game of Thrones, adding to its sight-seeing list the various shooting locales for both visitors and Game of Thrones enthusiasts.

Transportation Facilities to and from the airports to the heart of the city

There are a numerous options to choose from for reaching the Belfast city centre from the airports. Often, the commutes follow the same routes for both the airports, however, in some cases, they do not. Thus, it would be advisable for tourists to take notice of the schedule and routes of the transportation facilities meticulously.

- **By bus**

Translink, a bus service facility administered by the Northern Ireland's public commute service authority runs from both the airports to the city centre. However, the Translink service from the George Best Belfast City Airport follows route number 300 while the one plying from Belfast International Airport takes route number 600 to reach the city proper. The fares of the two different routes differ and thus it is advisable to check the website of Translink for getting updated information.

- **By car**

Several car rental authorities operate from both the airports where one gets convenience of parking. If the traffic system favours, it must take more than 20 minutes to reach the city centre from the domestic airport and in case of travelling by car from the international airport, it must not take more than 45 minutes to reach the city in light traffic.

- **By taxi**

Visitors may choose to hire taxis from the airports as a range of trustworthy local companies like Fonacabs or Value Cabs are available at their service.

Places in Belfast that must be visited

Belfast is an unavoidable muse for literature and fantasy lovers, for it inspired C.S. Lewis and Jonathan Swift to compose the *Chronicles of Narnia* and the *Gulliver's Travels* respectively and of course for Game of Thrones lovers for being a chief shooting locale for the series. This intriguing fact certainly does not imply that visitors who do not nurture their inclination in the same would not find the city worthy of visiting, for Belfast pledges to offer everyone something or the other. This pristine northern Irish city is an overwhelming tourist spot being a home to several significant landmarks like the Belfast City Hall, Ulster Museum, Titanic Belfast and so on.

Titanic Belfast

Belfast, at a stone's throw from the heart of the city, offers visitors an unforgettable maritime experience making other global cities envious. Titanic Belfast is the birth venue of the magnificent and colossal RMS Titanic and has as many as nine unique galleries where one would learn and experience from the self-guided tour of the famous ocean liner through various interactions of sights, sounds and smell. Titanic Belfast has honourably bagged the World's Leading Tourist Attraction Award with pride.

Titanic Studio and the Game of Thrones Experience

The name, Game of Thrones is a mention enough to stir the curiosity of the fandom. Whether be it the ever frozen Wall or the gay meadows of Riverrun, or perhaps, the snow white Winterfell or even the city centre of King's Landing, Belfast, along with other Northern Irish locales has catered to beautify and incarnate the story from the black and white pages to the silver screen. The Titanic Studio is thus not only a mere studio but a lifetime experience that one may proudly don as an achievement.

Ulster Museum

The Ulster Museum is a melange of art, science and history, bringing together under one roof, impressive collections of artefacts from the past to the present. It offers free visits to tourists and is one the chief gems in the crown of Northern Ireland. The museum remains open from Tuesday to Sunday, between 10:00 hours and 17:00 hours and remains closed on Mondays.

The Giant's Causeway

The Giant's Causeway is a mysterious tourist spot, not only because of its noteworthy and distinguishable geological feature but also for the uncanny legend centring the mythical giant, Finn McCool. The Giant's Causeway is a rugged terrain across the sea edge on the North Eastern coastline of Country Antrim and proudly stands with its basalt columns. This place has been maintained with great care being termed as one of the heritage sites of the world by UNESCO.

Hillsborough Castle and Gardens

The Hillsborough Castle along with its sprawling gardens is Georgian architecture with its characteristic and quaint features of the Georgian era as depicted by the Throne Room or the stark waterways beside the neatly trimmed lush gardens. At present, the castle is the official address of the royal family when they are on a visit to Northern Ireland. The castle has also been a prestigious residence of the Secretary of State for the past few decades since the 1970s.

Crumlin Road Gaol

The Crumlin Road Gaol has served as a Grade-A jail to the state for 150 years since 1846 and imparts a goose bump rousing vibe to visitors with its drab ambience. The Gaol on the Crumlin Road along with a grave yard, hospital, Hanging Cell and several other landmarks is connected with the courthouse by a tunnel. Presently, the Gaol also hosts majestic and eventful occasions and concerts.

Chapter 8 - Birmingham

About the city

Birmingham is the cradle of 18th century Enlightenment and one of the chief centres of the famous Industrial Revolution and thus the city is brimming with historical landmarks which must not go amiss on a visit. Birmingham, located on the river Rea in the province of West Midlands in England, is the most populous metropolitan borough, apart from London, in the country covering an area of about 589.9 square kilometres urban areas at an elevation of 460 ft. Being a significant region to inspire the movement of the Enlightenment, Birmingham has won accolades being referred and revered as the seat of Midlands Enlightenment or West Midlands Enlightenment or even Birmingham Enlightenment.

The residence to globally deferred personalities like James Wyatt, Erasmus Darwin, Anna Seward and others, the city stands with lofty pride nurturing the world famous Victoria Square, The St. Paul's Square and many other significant landmarks; the memorably lip-smacking chocolaty tour organized by the second largest confectionary brand, Cadbury in the self-guided exhibition cum tour inside the Cadbury World makes the city even more special and extraordinary. Besides, the city is also recognized for its evolutionary concepts of Tennis and Football leagues, being the home of the famous Birmingham City Football Club.

Travelling to and from the Birmingham International Airport to the city centre

One may reach the city centre of Birmingham effortlessly owing to the hassle free transportation system that the city maintains. Visitors may choose from the options of cars, taxis, coaches, buses and train to reach their destined city. The city is about 8 miles away from the Birmingham International Airport, which is on the eastern side of the city.

- **By bus**

Trustworthy bus services like the Megabus and Travel West Midlands are available at the convenience of visitors. Buses regularly ply every 20 minutes on weekday mornings and every 30 minutes on weekday evenings as well as Saturdays with the 900 Airport Link operating in between the Birmingham city centre and the passenger terminal at the airport.

- **By car**

Travelling by car is one of the most convenient options, for there is an impressive car parking facility provided by the authority of the airport at a reasonable rate. M6 and M42 are the routes advisable for travellers to drive their cars to reach the city centre.

- **By coach**

It is imperative for tourists who decide to travel by coaches to the Birmingham city centre from the passenger terminal to book the tickets beforehand due to its high demand. Reliable coach services like that of National Express, which provide with lucrative luggage allowances operate services covering long distances.

- **By train**

SkyRail, a free train service from the Birmingham International Airport to the Birmingham International Railway Station takes about 2 minutes to reach the rail hub. Trains running as regularly as 1 hour ply from the international station to the city centre at Birmingham New Street Station during the day, however, there are fewer trains evening onwards and none during the weekends.

Places to visit in Birmingham for certain

For a city that has bagged the position among the top 10 cities in the world to be visited according to the Rough's Guide, Birmingham does not need further enhancement in praise. The city has also been mentioned to be listed in the global tour list by both the New Yorker and The New York Times. The city, besides noteworthy landmarks also houses several four Michelin Star restaurants and also shopping arcades.

Victoria Square

The Victoria Square is the residence of both the Council houses as well as the Town Hall and is very close to the Chamberlain Square. It is considered to be the almost centrally located pedestrian square in the city networking the entire city via different roads and routes. For instance, it links the Bull's Ring and the areas of the Brindleyplace zones. The nomenclature of the square signifies tribute to the notable queen, Victoria and this central location is also the confluence of the major roads: Paradise Street, Colmore Road and the New Street.

The Cathedral Church of St. Phillip

Located on Colmore Road, this 18th century Baroque style cathedral church has several attributes of honor up its sleeves; it is not only the residence of the Bishop of Birmingham but also the Church of England Cathedral and has been serving as the Diocese of Birmingham since 1905. The cathedral has been witness to both the Industrial Revolution as well as The World War II when they was mercilessly bombed.

Bournville Centre of Visual Art

The Bournville Centre of Visual Art, also known as the Bournville College of Art and the Bournville School of Art, is located in the model village of Bournville in Birmingham. It not only houses the famous International Project Space but also hosts several exhibitions of contemporary as well as visual art by the college students. This college has several eminent personalities in its alumni list, like: Marjorie Yates, John Shelley, Donald Rodney, etc.

Cadbury World

The very tag 'Cadbury' is a description enough to describe the self-guided tour cum exhibition by this notable confectionary brand. The venue offers a detailed seventy five minute factory tour during the weekdays and a shortened tour during the weekends. This place is a favorite of all age groups of visitors get to view the world's largest waterfall, besides, they are also offered freshly liquefied gourmet chocolate during the tour inside the factory.

Great Britain

National SEA LIFE Centre, Birmingham

Opposite to the Barclaycard Arena and beside the Birmingham Canal Navigation Main Line Canal in Brindleyplace, the National SEA LIFE Centre, Birmingham is a marvelous and giant aquarium with a capacity of about one million litres of water. It houses several rare marine species while conserving them such as: Zebra Sharks, Sea Turtles, Gentoo Penguins, Blacktip Reef Sharks and so on. This venue is keen on breeding endangered species like the seahorses and is the sole completely transparent underwater tunnel with a 360 degree panoramic view. The authority advises to book tickets online to save a great deal and yet, enjoy the marine kingdom of 2000 sea creatures, known and unknown.

Chapter 9 - Glasgow

About the city

The Celtic city, Glasgow is a metropolis of style, sophistication and splendour; from the rich historical legacies to the modern evolutionary prospects, the city has abundant treasures to offer the tourists. This impressive conurbation evokes vibes of happiness and contentment through its pompous demeanour and sheer brilliance. The city houses more than 20 significant museums like Kelvingrove Art Gallery, the Burrell Collections and so on. Glasgow is also cherished as 'the UNESCO city of Music' and hence, one can effortlessly understand how flourished the city is culturally and a visitor might get baffled to choose from hundreds of clubs and pubs hosting esteemed musical events of which King Tut's Wah Wah Hut deserves special mention. Not only with the rich cultural heritage, this Scottish city buzzes with its amiable ambience along with the enriching provision of higher education in one of the top universities of the world, the University of Glasgow.

Travelling to and from the Glasgow Airport to the city centre

The airport at Glasgow is the only airport in the nation and thus, it just not is the only mean to reach the city centre but also to travel to any part of Scotland, if one is visiting from a foreign nation. The Glasgow Airport is about 8 miles away from the city centre and lies on the western side of it. There are several ways and means to reach the city with utmost convenience.

- ***Travelling by bus***

Bus is the most convenient and easiest means of commute to start off for the city centre. Starting from the bus stop at airport the buses duly arrive at the Buchanan Bus Station from where one would have innumerable options to travel throughout the city as well as the country. There are several bus service options running from the airport, as: First Glasgow Airport Service 500, Citylink 915, Citylink 977, First 77Hospital Connect and others. Some of these bus services provide the passengers with free Wi-Fi connection and mobile charging facility and takes as roughly as 15 minutes to reach the destination.

- ***Travelling by trains***

To travels by train one has to take a bus service to the nearest railway station, Paisley Gilmour Street to travel across the city. Detailed information must be secured from the websites like: ScotRail, Traveline Scotland etc.

- ***Travelling by taxi***

To travel by taxi, visitors must pre-book such services beforehand in order to avoid a last minute humdrum regarding the availability of taxis.

- ***Travelling by cycling or on foot***

Glasgow has a unique feature of travelling, i.e. one may reach the city centre on foot as there are well maintained footpaths for pedestrians. Besides, the authorities have also set up a National Cycle Networks for adventure enthusiastic cyclists.

Must visit places for sightseers

Elected and revered in 1999 as 'The UK's City of Architecture and Design', Glasgow is a modern civilization booming in elegance with great leaps. Be it speciality museums or art museums, the recollections of the Scottish Enlightenment or that of the Scottish Industrial Revolution, the merchant city of Glasgow is a heavenly destinations for sightseers. Again, it is the chosen spot for shopaholics in the UK after London.

The Riverside Museum of Transport and Travel

Visitors who have a knack for exploring vintage vehicles and other means of technology driven vehicles, it is imperative that they drop here by hook or crook. This museum conducts self-guided tours exhibiting steam engines, the world's oldest cycle, vintage cars, vintage Celtic buses and trolleys and trams, etc.

Kelvingrove Art Gallery and Museum

Kelvingrove Art Gallery and Museum is the most popular tourist destination in entire Scotland on the Argyle Street with about 22 thematic state –of –the –art display options along with about 8000 awe- inspiring exhibits satiating the tourists' minds for years.

King's Theatre

Located at the confluence of the Bath Street and Elmbank Street, the King's Theatre is the platform of several upcoming theatrical groups along with the renowned ones. A string of musical events, opera, and dance recitals along with circus-like performances are hosted year. The First Family Productions arranges for an annual pantomime every year on the stage of this popular theatre.

King Tut's Wah Wah Hut

The King Tut's Wah Wah Hut is one of the chief venues of live musical performances along with the provisions of a bar. King Tut's Wah Wah Hut is the most popular hanging out destination for enjoying and appreciating esteemed and tasteful Scottish comedy, music, performing arts respectively.

Provand's Lordship

The Provand's Lordship is a medial period house that has been transformed into a museum for public benefit. This house overviews several of the priceless landmarks of Glasgow like: Glasgow Royal Infirmary, Glasgow Cathedral, St. Mungo Museum of Religious Life Art and many others. This historical building was built in 1471 as a significant wing of St. Nicholas Hospital by The Bishop of Glasgow and was later transformed into a museum.

Church of Scotland

The Church of Scotland is the national church of the country and is a brilliant specimen of the Reformation era in the Celtic zone. Protestantism and Presbyterianism is religiously practiced in here and is popularly known as the Kirk in the local Scottish dialect. This church is the witness to the evolution of Christian principles in the Scottish domain in about 1560. This church protects and maintains the principles and drawings of the revolutionary Protestant leader, John Calvin.

Glasgow Botanic Gardens

Built in 1817, the Glasgow Botanic Gardens is the home to several magnificent floras and well maintained glass houses. The Kibble Palace is the chief centre of attraction within the premises of the garden exhibiting many cutting edge sculptures. This garden, which was once served by a railway line, nurtures an endless list of trees and plants, including rare ferns and carnivorous plants.

Glasgow Necropolis

Built on the east of Glasgow Cathedral, the Glasgow Necropolis is a Victorian cemetery sheltering as many as 3500 monuments including the famous tombs of Mrs Lockhart and William Motherwell along with the ones of the martyrs of World War I and World War II respectively.

Conclusion

The United Kingdom of The Great Britain and northern Ireland is filled with exotic places and most tempting tourist destinations which has made at one of the most favorite countries for holiday destinations. Comprising of Scotland Wales Northern Ireland and England the UK is white awfully referred as "GB" which stands for the Great Britain. This country appeals to all the people living on this planet due to its rich culture and diversifying landscape sceneries. This beautiful country and its people have done a fantastic job in preserving the heritage as well as the well maintained castles and estates along with monumental landmarks are extremely popular and World renowned museum and art galleries.

Exploring this country which is one of the topmost in the list of the most beautiful countries on this planet is honestly one of the greatest happiness that a person can enjoy. Going on a vacation in the UK and checking out cities such as London, Liverpool and Birmingham will make you sweep off your feet and make you realize how beautiful this world is. The entire United Kingdom is well connected and places in this country are easily accessible by means of train or bus ride from one place to another. This is a blessing for the tourists as they can cover this entire country easily and enjoy each moment of it.

Once you have started travelling the whole of the United Kingdom then get ready and all set to explore the four Nations you will soon find out that these Nations differ from one another in various aspects. The people and the culture of these Nations a separate from each other along with the religion, food customs and last but not the least the accents. You will find exotic force lines located in the Southwest region of England, along with green rolling hills all around you, besides the Premier League games which occurs in the top most cities

Great Britain

of Britain which are Manchester and Liverpool, flooded by football fans all round the year. Apart from the iconic scene of the London Skyline which you will see from above the Tower Bridge The Great Britain has an impressive and extensive collection of antiques and artifacts in the museums which are located here.

It is quite truly said that the history of the United Kingdom is synced together with the modern culture and makes this place a paradise for both the lovers of natures as well the seekers of modern norms and culture. Right from the hustle bustle of the city, to the serene beauty of the countryside, from the sensational nightlife to the historical and cozy towns and villages – the Great Britain and its parts have it all in store for you to explore. So what are you waiting for? Visit this country and feel the experience of a lifetime.

Printed in Poland
by Amazon Fulfillment
Poland Sp. z o.o., Wrocław